Tug and the Bug

by Liza Charlesworth • illustrated by Doug Jones

SCHOLASTIC INC.

New York • Toronto • London • Auckland
Sydney • Mexico City • New Delhi • Hong Kong

No part of this publication may be reproduced, stored in a retrieval system, or transmitted in any form or by any means, electronic, mechanical, photocopying, recording, or otherwise, without written permission of the publisher. For information regarding permission, write to Scholastic Inc., Attention: Permissions Department, 557 Broadway, New York, NY 10012.

Designed by Grafica, Inc.
ISBN: 978-0-545-68626-6
Copyright © 2009 by Lefty's Editorial Services.
All rights reserved. Published by Scholastic Inc.
SCHOLASTIC, LET'S LEARN READERS™, and associated logos are trademarks and/or registered trademarks of Scholastic Inc.

12 11 10 9 8 7 6 5 4 3 2 1   68   15 16 17 18 19 20/0

Printed in China.

What Is a Word Family?
A word family is a group of words that rhyme and share the same spelling pattern, such as *Tug, bug,* and *pug.* Read this story to learn more *-ug* words!

This is **Tug**.
Tug is a member of the **Ug** family.

One day, **Tug** was playing with his **pug** when he met a friendly **bug**.

The **bug** asked **Tug**
to help him find a **snug** home.

"How about this **jug**?" asked **Tug**.
"Too dark," said the **bug**.

"How about this **mug**?" asked **Tug**.
"Too small," said the **bug**.

"How about this hole I **dug**?" asked **Tug**.
"Too dirty," said the **bug**.

"How about this box?" asked **Tug**.
"Too crowded," said the **bug**.

You see, the box belonged
to a slimy **slug**.

Tug and the **bug** sat down on an old **rug**.
"Will I ever find a home?" asked the **bug**.
Tug gave a sad **shrug**.

Then the **bug** had a great idea!
"This **rug** is soft, warm, and cozy.
It's the perfect home!"

Tug and the **pug** helped the **bug**
lug the **rug** to the yard.

Then he lived happily ever after,
snug as a **bug** in a **rug**!

Word Family House

Point to the *-ug* word in each room and read it aloud.

dug　　hug　　jug

rug　　lug　　mug

pug　　bug　　chug

plug　　　　slug

snug　　　　shrug

Word Family Riddles

Read each *-ug* riddle. Then point to the answer in the word box.

1 I am an insect.

2 You drink out of me.

3 I am what a train does.

4 I am a kind of dog.

5 I mean *cozy*.

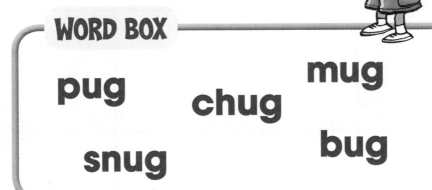

WORD BOX

pug

chug

mug

snug

bug

Answers: 1. bug 2. mug 3. chug 4. pug 5. snug

Word Family Bingo

Which words belong to the -ug family? Cover them with buttons or pennies. Get four in a row to win!

mug	chin	spot	chug
clam	snug	will	lug
snack	tin	tot	hug
back	chill	bug	pug

Answer: Bingo is the fourth column down: chug, lug, hug, pug.